THE OFFICIAL
ASTON VILLA
ANNUAL 2008

Compiled by Rob Bishop and Tricia Mills

Special thanks to Gayner Monkton, Lorna McClelland
and Neville Williams Photography

A Grange Publication

© 2007. Published by Grange Communications Ltd., Edinburgh under licence
from Aston Villa Football Club plc. Printed in the EU.

ISBN 978-1-905426-78-2

£6.99

CLUB HONOURS

EUROPEAN CUP
Winners: 1982
Quarter-finalists: 1982-83

EUROPEAN SUPER CUP
Winners: 1982-83

WORLD CLUBS CHAMPIONSHIP
Runners-up: 1982

INTERTOTO CUP
Winners: 2001

FOOTBALL LEAGUE
Champions: 1893-94, 1895-96, 1896-97, 1898-99,
 1899-1900, 1909-10, 1980-81
Runners-up: 1888-89, 1902-03, 1907-08, 1910-11, 1912-13,
1913-14, 1930-31, 1932-33, 1989-90

PREMIERSHIP
Runners-up: 1992-93

DIVISION TWO
Champions: 1937-38, 1959-60

DIVISION THREE
Champions: 1971-72

FA CUP
Winners: 1887, 1895, 1897, 1905, 1913,
1920, 1957
Runners-up: 1892, 1924, 2000

LEAGUE CUP
Winners: 1961, 1975, 1977, 1994, 1996
Runners-up: 1963, 1971

FA YOUTH CUP
Winners: 1972, 1980, 2002
Runners-up: 2004

CONTENTS

SEASON REVIEW STARTS ON PAGE 7

SPOT THE DIFFERENCE ON PAGE 43

CRAIG GARDNER THE LOCAL
LAD ON PAGE 34

JOHN
CAREW

Season Review 06-07

Around 1,000 supporters gather at Villa Park to welcome former Leicester City and Celtic boss Martin O'Neill as the club's new manager following the departure of David O'Leary. O'Neill receives a tumultuous welcome on the evening of Friday 3rd August and it's straight down to work the following day as he jets off to Hanover to take charge of the team in their pre-season tour of Germany and Holland.

His influence is immediately apparent as Villa kick off the Premiership campaign with an excellent point in a 1-1 draw against Arsenal. Central defender Olof Mellberg has the distinction of scoring the first goal at the Gunners' new Emirates Stadium, located barely half a mile from Arsenal's former Highbury home.

Four days later, Villa recover from going a goal behind to beat Premiership new boys Reading 2-1. The Royals had been 3-2 winners over Middlesbrough on the opening day so this is their first

OLOF MELLBERG CELEBRATES WITH HIS TEAM MATES AFTER HIS GOAL AGAINST ARSENAL

> " LAST SEASON WE WERE OFTEN IN CONTROL OF GAMES AND THEN CONCEDED SILLY GOALS BUT AT ARSENAL IT WAS TOTALLY DIFFERENT. WE DEFENDED WELL AND IT WAS A GOOD ALL-ROUND TEAM PERFORMANCE "
> **OLOF MELLBERG**

defeat in Premiership football. Juan Pablo equalises from the penalty spot after Luke Moore has been fouled, and newly-appointed skipper Gareth Barry heads home a Peter Whittingham cross for the winner.

It gets better still the following Sunday. Just before the match, it's announced that Barry has signed a new four-year contract and as if to celebrate, Moore opens the scoring inside two minutes!

A well-taken goal from Angel makes it 2-0 by the 38th minute and that's how it stays.

Just as the transfer window closes, Villa sign Bulgarian midfielder Stiliyan Petrov from Celtic for £6.5m

The early indications are that life under Martin O'Neill is going to be enjoyable!

JUAN PABLO ANGEL ON HIS WAY TO SCORING VILLA'S SECOND GOAL

Premiership position: **2**nd

SEPTEMBER

Five matches, no defeats. The month of September is another one to savour for the claret and blue faithful – particularly as only one of the games is at Villa Park.

Stiliyan Petrov enjoys an outstanding debut in a 1-1 draw against West Ham at Upton Park and is desperately unlucky not to score when he flicks the ball over goalkeeper Roy Carroll, only to see Tyrone Mears make an acrobatic clearance from under the bar. Villa are ahead through Liam Ridgewell after only four minutes, Bobby Zamora equalising for the

Hammers early in the second half.

There's a 0-0 stalemate against newly-promoted Watford at Vicarage Road before Villa take the first step along the Carling Cup trail by beating Scunthorpe United at Glanford Park. It's a tricky tie against the battling League One side but two goals from Juan Pablo Angel – one of them from a rebound after goalkeeper Joe Murphy had saved his penalty – see O'Neill's men through to the third round.

In the only home game of the month, Villa supporters salute a magnificent goal by Gabby Agbonlahor in a 2-0 victory over Charlton Athletic, the youngster from Erdington firing a close-range volley into the top corner following a cross from Gareth Barry.

JUAN PABLO ANGEL SCORES AT SCUNTHORPE

PETROV DEBUT AGAINST WEST HAM'S YOSSI BENAYOUN

Luke Moore nets the other goal in the second half, but Agbonlahor is undoubtedly Villa's man of the moment.

At Stamford Bridge a week later, he has the satisfaction of scoring against Chelsea, netting with a glancing header after Ridgewell heads a Steven Davis centre back across goal. Gabby's goal earns a 1-1 draw against Jose Mourinho's men and leaves Villa unbeaten in eight matches. The downside is that Moore badly damages his shoulder and is told he will be out of action for up to four months.

> " MY CONFIDENCE IS GROWING GAME BY GAME AND I FEEL I'M DEVELOPING AS A PLAYER. THE MANAGER ENCOURAGES US TO GO OUT AND EXPRESS OURSELVES AND THAT HELPS A LOT "
> GABBY AGBONLAHOR

Premiership position: **6**th

DIDIER DROGBA HAS NO CHANCE AGAINST HIGH FLIER THOMAS SORENSEN

OCTOBER

Gareth Barry, who grew up as a Tottenham supporter, scores one of the finest goals of his career to earn a point in a 1-1 home draw against his boyhood favourites.

Controlling Stiliyan Petrov's pass, he twists and turns his way past Paul Stalteri and Jermaine Jenas before sending a right foot shot into the far top corner from the left hand edge of the penalty area.

Villa have gone behind in bizarre circumstances. Barely a minute after wasting the chance to open the scoring with a penalty which he blazes over the bar, Juan Pablo Angel has dropped back into defence to help out at a corner – and has headed the ball into his own net!

That's the second time Angel has failed from the spot, so when Villa are awarded another penalty at home to Fulham a week later, Barry takes over, driving his spot kick past goalkeeper Antti Nieimi and into the top left hand corner. The skipper's goal gives Villa a 25th minute lead, but German midfielder Moritz Voltz earns the Cottagers a 1-1 draw with an equaliser on the stroke of half-time.

Next up are Leicester City in the third round of the Carling Cup, and it turns out to be a marathon against the Foxes at the Walkers Stadium. Behind after only four minutes, Villa are quickly level through Angel, with Barry firing home a penalty just before half-time to put the visitors ahead. But after Leicester draw level near the end, the captain has a second penalty saved by goalkeeper Paul Henderson in stoppage time. The tie goes into extra-time, and a penalty shoot-out looks increasingly likely to settle the outcome until Gabby Agbonlahor strikes home an angled half-volley

GABBY AGBONLAHOR AND PASCAL CHIMBONDA JUMP HIGH FOR THE BALL

in the 119th minute.

Gabby is also on target at Anfield the following Saturday but it's not enough to prevent a 3-1 defeat by Liverpool. Villa's 11-match unbeaten start to the season is over.

GABBY CONGRATULATES HIS TEAM MATE

> " THERE WAS PLENTY OF BANTER IN THE BARRY HOUSEHOLD AFTER THE SPURS GAME. TWO OF MY THREE BROTHERS ARE DIEHARD TOTTENHAM FANS AND THEY WERE CALLING ME A FEW NAMES AFTER MY GOAL! "
> **GARETH BARRY**

Premiership position: **7**th

NOVEMBER

Veteran striker Chris Sutton was signed the previous month as cover during Luke Moore's absence, and the former Blackburn Rovers and Celtic striker really makes his presence felt during the early weeks of November.

His excellent performance is the highlight of a 2-0 home win over Blackburn Rovers, even though the goalscoring honours are shared by Gareth Barry – from yet another penalty – and Juan Pablo Angel.

Seven days later, Sutton claims his first goal in claret and blue, beating Everton goalkeeper Tim Howard with a deft header from Isaiah Osbourne's centre as Villa win 1-0 at Goodison Park. The match on Merseyside marks the return to action of young central defender Gary Cahill, who had been sidelined by injury sustained on the club's pre-season tour.

In between the two league victories over Blackburn and Everton, there's a reality check in the form of a 4-0 Carling Cup thrashing by Chelsea. Even so, around 6,000 fans make the trip to Stamford Bridge, many of them tempted by the club's offer of free transport, creating a carnival atmosphere at Chelsea's famous Shed End.

After the excellent win at Everton, Martin O'Neill's men have to settle for draws away to Wigan Athletic (0-0) and at home to Middlesbrough (1-1), Barry salvaging a point against the Teessiders with a penalty on the stroke of half-time.

But the month ends on a disappointing note, Villa slipping to a 3-1 midweek home defeat at the hands of Manchester City, the only consolation being a rare goal from midfielder Gavin McCann.

Czech Republic midfielder Patrik Berger, meanwhile, joins Championship club Stoke City on loan.

ABOVE: CHRIS SUTTON LEAPS INTO ACTION TRYING THE ACROBATIC APPROACH… BELOW: VILLA'S STRONG DEFENSIVE WALL

GAVIN McCANN HAMMERS VILLA'S CONSOLATION GOAL AGAINST CITY

Premiership position: 5th

> " THE BUZZ AMONG THE FANS IS DEFINITELY SHARED BY THE PLAYERS AND STAFF. IT GIVES US AN EXTRA DETERMINATION TO DO WELL, KNOWING THAT EVERYONE IS PULLING IN THE SAME DIRECTION " THOMAS SORENSEN

STILIYAN PETROV CELEBRATES
HIS FIRST GOAL FOR VILLA

It seems Villa are becoming the draw specialists of the Premiership – at least until the middle of the month, when things start to go horribly wrong.

> " IT'S GREAT TO SCORE MY FIRST GOAL IN THE PREMIERSHIP AND IT MEANS A LOT TO ME. I CAN REMEMBER MY FIRST GOAL FOR CELTIC AND IT WILL BE THE SAME WITH THIS ONE "
> STILIYAN PETROV

It's good to see Juan Pablo Angel and former Villa goalkeeper David James exchanging shirts after the 2-2 draw against Portsmouth at Fratton Park. After all, they were good pals during their time together at Villa Park, and Angel has now scored past James while the keeper has been playing for West Ham, Manchester City and Portsmouth.

GABBY AGBONLAHOR CHALLENGES SOL CAMPBELL

GABBY CLOSES IN ON EDWIN VAN DER SAR

This latest goal earns a point after the home side have cancelled out a first half penalty conversion by Gareth Barry.

The outcome against Sheffield United at Bramall Lane is also 2-2, and the scoring follows the same pattern as the Portsmouth match.

Stiliyan Petrov's first goal for Villa gives the visitors a second minute lead, only for the Blades to hit back after half-time and establish a 2-1 advantage. But within 60 seconds of Danny Webber putting United ahead, Milan Baros drives home the equaliser which earns Villa a deserved point.

Unfortunately, goalkeeper Stuart Taylor suffers a knee injury at Bramall Lane, and with Thomas Sorensen already sidelined, Villa are forced to make the emergency loan signing of Crystal Palace's Gabor Kiraly.

It's not exactly a happy festive season for Kiraly, Villa going down 1-0 to Bolton Wanderers and 3-0 to Manchester United on home soil before rounding off the year with two fruitless trips to London. Gareth Barry is on target against both Tottenham Hotspur and Charlton Athletic, his goal at The Valley coming from yet another penalty, but Villa lose both matches 2-1.

Premiership position: **12**th

11

After a depressing sequence of four straight defeats, Villa have every reason to be delighted at holding mighty Chelsea to a goalless draw at Villa Park in the televised New Year Bank Holiday game.

Unfortunately they are unable to maintain the momentum in the FA Cup against Manchester United at Old Trafford the following Sunday. There seems to be every possibility of a replay when Milan Baros cancels out Henrik Larsson's opening goal for United and the teams are still level going into stoppage time. But Gabor Kiraly allows Ole Gunnar Solskjaer's shot to slip through his fingers and Martin O'Neill's side are out of the competition.

Baros produces another inspired piece of football when Villa head back to Old Trafford for a league match six days later, brilliantly setting up a goal for Gabby Agbonlahor. But there is no prospect of a dramatic finale this time around – United have gone three-up by the 35th minute and Gabby's goal is merely a consolation in a comprehensive 3-1 defeat.

United full-back Phil Bardsley,

who joined Villa on loan in between the two games, makes his debut as Villa record their first win of 2007 the following week. This time it's Villa's turn to dish out a helping of late heartache. The game is heading towards a goalless draw until their Gavin (Mahon) deflects a shot from our Gavin (McCann) into his own net four minutes from time. A second goal right at the end from Agbonlahor secures a 2-0 verdict which had barely looked possible a few minutes earlier.

There's plenty of transfer activity around this time. Ashley Young signs from Watford in a deal worth an initial £8m, while John Carew arrives from French club Lyon with Baros moving in the opposite direction.

The two new boys both make their debuts in a midweek match against Newcastle United at St. James' Park and immediately strike up a good understanding. Young marks his first appearance for Villa with a goal, while Carew hits the post and has an effort disallowed. Despite dominating the game though, O'Neill's men somehow lose 3-1, their cause not being helped when they concede two goals in the opening seven minutes!

Even as the action is taking place on Tyneside, Celtic midfielder Shaun Maloney is completing a £1m deadline day transfer which is completed just a few minutes before midnight.

ASHLEY YOUNG IS CONGRATULATED BY HIS TEAM MATES

" I'M REALLY HAPPY TO BE AT A CLUB WHICH HAS AMBITIONS OF BEING IN THE TOP SIX AND GETTING INTO EUROPE "
ASHLEY YOUNG

Premiership position: 14th

JOHN CAREW SCORES

> " IF I COULD HAVE CHOSEN BETWEEN SCORING IN MY FIRST GAME AND MY SECOND, I WOULD HAVE GONE FOR THE SECOND – BECAUSE IT WAS MY FIRST GAME AT HOME "
> **JOHN CAREW**

There were five games in January, with half a dozen scheduled for April. But February and March are barren from a Villa point of view.

During the course of two months, Martin O'Neill's men play just five games. At one stage, in fact, they go five-and-a-half weeks between home fixtures – then play twice at Villa Park in the space of five days!

The new boys become instant heroes on their home debuts, Ashley Young providing the pass from which John Carew fires home the only goal of the game against West Ham.

Villa are full value for all three points, controlling the game from start to finish without being able to build on their 36th minute lead. But right at the death, the Hammers burst into life, forcing Thomas Sorensen into a couple of late saves.

A week later, Shaun Maloney shows some promising touches on his first appearance for the club against Reading at the Madejski Stadium but it's an afternoon when nothing goes right for Martin O'Neill's men. Despite creating a succession of openings, they slip to a 2-0 defeat.

After a three-week break without any sort of action, Villa collect a point from a 1-1 draw against Fulham at Craven Cottage, where Carew is again on target. The Norwegian striker, though, is booked for celebrating with Villa's travelling army of 5,000 supporters, who have completely taken over the Putney End.

Back at Villa Park after an extended absence, Villa go down 1-0 at home to Arsenal in a midweek match before drawing 0-0 against Liverpool in a strangely subdued contest the following Sunday.

ASHLEY YOUNG TACKLES DIRK KUYT

JOHN CAREW DISPLAYS HIS PACE AGAINST FULHAM

Premiership position: **13**th

April showers? It's raining away wins!

Villa have only won once on their Premiership travels all season, and that was back in November at Everton. But how that situation changes as they record three away wins on the trot during April!

Indeed, it's the best sequence of league away results since 1998, when John Gregory's side finished the season with five straight away successes.

through ball sets up Gabby Agbonlahor for the winner.

At the end of the game, Villa's ecstatic players go over to the Darwen End to celebrate with around 4,000 fans who have made the trip. The win is so welcome that some of them even throw their shirts into the crowd!

The team also fall behind at Middlesbrough a week later, but Craig Gardner nets his first Villa goal to bring the scores level on the stroke of half-time before

PATRIK BERGER SETS THE BALL ROLLING

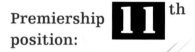

CRAIG GARDNER CELEBRATES

> " I HADN'T REALLY THOUGHT ABOUT SCORING MY FIRST GOAL BUT IT WAS NICE TO GET ONE AT LAST "
> SHAUN MALONEY

You can sense both the relief and delight among the players as their long run of disappointment comes to an end against Blackburn Rovers at Ewood Park on Easter Saturday.

It looks like being the same old story when Benni McCarthy fires Rovers into a 24th minute lead. But Patrik Berger, making his first starting appearance for Villa for 18 months, is in inspirational mood, flicking home a 35th minute equaliser (his first goal for the club) before his magnificent

JOHN CAREW SCORES AT EASTLANDS

Luke Moore and Stiliyan Petrov complete a 3-1 victory.

Shaun Maloney then joins the list of new Villa goalscorers, netting his first for the club with a dipping free-kick in a 2-0 win at Manchester City, John Carew having headed us into the lead.

While the team pick up maximum points away from home, they have to settle for three draws at Villa Park. Agbonlahor's second half equalisers earn 1-1 results against Everton and Wigan, while the game against Portsmouth finishes goalless.

Premiership position: **11**th

What a spectacular finish to the home programme! Every Villa supporter in a final day capacity crowd is given a free scarf, proclaiming the club's brand message: "Proud history – bright future."

It works wonders, too. Martin O'Neill's men produce some of their best form of the season, cutting through Sheffield United's defence time after time.

Gabby Agbonlahor and Ashley Young establish a two-goal half-time lead before Patrik Berger completes an emphatic 3-0 victory with a superb effort which is later voted Villa's Goal of the Season.

A week later at the Reebok Stadium, Villa twice trail to Bolton but hit back on each occasion for a 2-2 draw which

means they have finished the season unbeaten in nine matches. Craig Gardner and Luke Moore are the players on target, both with excellent volleys.

> " IT DOESN'T REALLY MATTER WHO SCORES THE GOALS OR WHAT THEY LOOK LIKE. BUT IT'S NICE TO GIVE THE FANS SOMETHING SPECIAL EVERY NOW AND THEN "
> PATRIK BERGER

Premiership position: **11**th

Final Table

TEAM	P	HOME					AWAY					Pts
		W	D	L	F	A	W	D	L	F	A	
1. Manchester United	38	15	2	2	46	12	13	3	3	37	15	89
2. Chelsea	38	12	7	0	37	11	12	4	3	27	13	83
3. Liverpool	38	14	4	1	39	7	6	4	9	18	20	68
4. Arsenal	38	12	6	1	43	16	7	5	7	20	19	68
5. Tottenham Hotspur	38	12	3	4	34	22	5	6	8	23	32	60
6. Everton	38	11	4	4	33	17	4	9	6	19	19	58
7. Bolton Wanderers	38	9	5	5	26	20	7	3	9	21	32	56
8. Reading	38	11	2	6	29	20	5	5	9	23	27	55
9. Portsmouth	38	11	5	3	28	15	3	7	9	17	27	54
10. Blackburn Rovers	38	9	3	7	31	25	6	4	9	21	29	52
11. ASTON VILLA	**38**	**7**	**8**	**4**	**20**	**14**	**4**	**9**	**6**	**23**	**27**	**50**
12. Middlesbrough	38	10	3	6	31	24	2	7	10	13	25	46
13. Newcastle United	38	7	7	5	23	20	4	3	12	15	27	43
14. Manchester City	38	5	6	8	10	16	6	3	10	19	28	42
15. West Ham	38	8	2	9	24	26	4	3	12	11	33	41
16. Fulham	38	7	7	5	18	18	1	8	10	20	42	39
17. Wigan Athletic	38	5	4	10	18	30	5	4	10	19	29	38
18. Sheffield United	38	7	6	6	24	21	3	2	14	8	34	38
19. Charlton Athletic	38	7	5	7	19	20	1	5	13	15	40	34
20. Watford	38	3	9	7	19	25	2	4	13	10	34	28

RESULTS AT A GLANCE

Date	Opponents	Result	Scorers
Aug 19	Arsenal	1-1	Mellberg
Aug 23	**READING**	**2-1**	**Angel pen, Barry**
Aug 27	**NEWCASTLE UNITED**	**2-0**	**Moore, Angel**
Sep 10	West Ham United	1-1	Ridgewell
Sep 16	Watford	0-0	
Sep 20	Scunthorpe United (LC2)	2-1	Angel 2
Sep 23	**CHARLTON ATHLETIC**	**2-0**	**Agbonlahor, Moore**
Sep 30	Chelsea	1-1	Agbonlahor
Oct 14	**TOTTENHAM HOTSPUR**	**1-1**	**Barry**
Oct 21	**FULHAM**	**1-1**	**Barry pen**
Oct 24	Leicester City (LC3)	3-2	Angel, Barry pen, Agbonlahor
Oct 28	Liverpool	1-3	Agbonlahor
Nov 5	**BLACKBURN ROVERS**	**2-0**	**Barry pen, Angel**
Nov 8	Chelsea (LC4)	0-4	
Nov 11	Everton	1-0	Sutton
Nov 19	Wigan Athletic	0-0	
Nov 25	**MIDDLESBROUGH**	**1-1**	**Barry pen**
Nov 29	**MANCHESTER CITY**	**1-3**	**McCann**
Dec 2	Portsmouth	2-2	Barry pen, Angel
Dec 11	Sheffield United	2-2	Petrov, Baros
Dec 16	**BOLTON WANDERERS**	**0-1**	
Dec 23	**MANCHESTER UNITED**	**0-3**	
Dec 26	Tottenham Hotspur	1-2	Barry
Dec 30	Charlton Athletic	1-2	Barry pen
Jan 2	**CHELSEA**	**0-0**	
Jan 7	Manchester United (FAC3)	1-2	Baros
Jan 13	Manchester United	1-3	Agbonlahor
Jan 20	**WATFORD**	**2-0**	**Mahon (og), Agbonlahor**
Jan 31	Newcastle United	1-3	Young
Feb 3	**WEST HAM UNITED**	**1-0**	**Carew**
Feb 10	Reading	0-2	
Mar 3	Fulham	1-1	Carew
Mar 14	**ARSENAL**	**0-1**	
Mar 18	**LIVERPOOL**	**0-0**	
Aprl 2	**EVERTON**	**1-1**	**Agbonalahor**
Aprl 7	Blackburn Rovers	2-1	Berger, Agbonalhor
Aprl 9	**WIGAN ATHLETIC**	**1-1**	**Agbonlahor**
Aprl 14	Middlesbrough	3-1	Gardner, Moore, Petrov
Aprl 22	**PORTSMOUTH**	**0-0**	
Aprl 28	Manchester City	2-0	Carew, Maloney
May 5	**SHEFFIELD UNITED**	**3-0**	**Agbonlahor, Young, Berger**
May 13	Bolton Wanderers	2-2	Gardner, Moore

ASHLEY YOUNG

True colours!

ABOVE: NEW SIGNING MARLON HAREWOOD WITH MARTIN O'NEILL

But rather than settle for the blue of the Latics, he jumped at the chance of sticking with the claret and blue shirt.

"I'm delighted to have joined Villa and I think I've come to the club at a really exciting time," says the former Nottingham Forest player.

"I want to recapture the form I showed a couple of seasons ago, when West Ham got to the FA Cup final and we did so well in the league."

Villa fans don't really want reminding of that. Harewood netted a hat-trick when the Hammers beat us

> ## " I'M DELIGHTED TO HAVE JOINED VILLA AND I THINK I'VE COME TO THE CLUB AT A REALLY EXCITING TIME "
> MARLON HAREWOOD

When footballers are transferred, they sometimes struggle to settle into their new surroundings. But that should be no problem for two of Villa's summer signings.

When midfielder Nigel Reo-Coker and striker Marlon Harewood pull on a claret and blue Villa shirt, it's just like they did at West Ham – the only other Barclays Premier League team who wear our famous colours.

Both players were big favourites at Upton Park, but both of them were absolutely delighted to head up the M1 to Villa Park when manager Martin O'Neill made bids for them.

Harewood, in fact, was on the brink of joining Wigan Athletic, and had even undergone a medical at the Lancashire club.

4-0 early in the season – and then rubbed it in by scoring a penalty when the Londoners completed a double with a 2-1 success at Villa Park.

Reo-Coker, meanwhile, insists he is no Big Time Charlie, despite the fact that he comes from London and that he has cost so much money. He is simply fulfilling a dream he nurtured as a young boy.

"Football is my occupation and I love the game," he says. "It's something I dreamed of doing from a young age. But I don't build myself up to be something I'm not. All I want to do is to be successful.

"I'm not a superstar or a miracle worker. I'm a hard-working person and I give 100 per cent in every game I play. The reason I joined this club is their aspiration to play in Europe. Martin O'Neill has told me what he is aiming to do and I believe we can achieve it."

Reo-Coker, who began his career with Wimbledon before making his name with West Ham, is certainly not been short of familiar faces as he has settled in at Villa Park. Apart from his former Hammers team-mate Harewood, he is also a friend of Ashley Young, who joined Villa from Watford during the January 2007 transfer window.

"When I found out Ashley had moved to Villa, I sent him a text to congratulate him," he says. "I said to him: 'Well done, you deserve it.'

"We also speak a lot on the phone and before I joined, he told me about the club and how much he was enjoying his time here. He told me all about the manger, the staff and the fans.

"I enjoyed every minute of my time at West Ham but this is a new chapter, a new beginning for me."

RIGHT: NEW SIGNING NIGEL REO-COKER

"I ENJOYED EVERY MINUTE OF MY TIME AT WEST HAM BUT THIS IS A NEW CHAPTER"
NIGEL REO-COKER

Gabby's gift for goals!

Scoring goals is second nature to Gabby Agbonlahor – no matter what level he is playing at.

He once scored 40 in one season for Villa's youth team and after stepping up to the reserves he was on target 13 times in as many games.

He also scored on his first team debut against Everton at Goodison Park – and followed up with 10 goals in his first full season to finish as the club's leading scorer. Here's a run-down of how he went to the top of Villa's scoring class.

1. CHARLTON ATHLETIC (h) 2-0

Skipper Gareth Barry sets up Gabby's fist goal of the season, accepting a short pass from Steven Davis before delivering a probing cross. Having given his marker the slip, Gabby is six yards out when he makes contact with the ball and his volley could not be better controlled or more sweetly struck as it flies past goalkeeper Scott Carson.

2. CHELSEA (a) 1-1

What a goal to savour – the equaliser in a draw with Jose Mourinho's mighty men at Stamford Bridge. Steven Davis, spotting Liam Ridgewell in space beyond the far post, delivers a perfect centre which the central defender heads back across goal for Gabby to score with a well-placed header past goalkeeper Petr Cech and into the bottom left hand corner.

3. LEICESTER CITY (a) 3-2

With only 90 seconds of extra-time remaining at the Walkers Stadium, a penalty shoot-out looks inevitable in this third round Carling Cup-tie. Gabby has other ideas. He latches on to a loose clearance and unleashes a powerful half volley which deflects past goalkeeper Paul Henderson for a dramatic Villa winner.

4. LIVERPOOL (a) 1-3

Gabby flicks a headed pass to Chris Sutton before moving on to an intelligent return ball from the former Celtic striker to fire clinically past Pepe Reina from 15 yards.

5. MANCHESTER UNITED (a) 1-3

Another consolation goal, this time at Old Trafford. It's one Gabby can hardly miss, the young striker driving the ball into the roof of the net from barely a yard following some clever footwork and an inviting low cross from Milan Baros.

GABBY CELEBRATES AS HE SCORES HIS SIXTH GOAL OF THE SEASON AGAINST WATFORD

GOAAAAAALLLLLL!

GABBY'S TO THE RESCUE WITH HIS LATE EXTRA-TIME WINNER AGAINST LEICESTER

6. WATFORD (h) 2-0

After Gavin McCann has played the ball forward to relieve a rare spell of Watford pressure, Gabby cashes in on a slip by Danny Shittu to dart through the middle before composing himself to slot a low 20-yard shot past the advancing Ben Foster.

7. EVERTON (h) 1-1

With Villa one-down, Gabby plays the ball into the goalmouth in the 83rd minute. Goalkeeper Tim Howard parries the ball at John Carew's feet, but Gabby calmly slots home the rebound to earn an important point.

8. BLACKBURN ROVERS (a) 2-1

Racing on to a superb through ball from Patrik Berger, Gabby displays great composure to slip past experienced goalkeeper Brad Friedel before rolling the ball into the net for a 74th minute winner.

9. WIGAN ATHLETIC (h) 1-1

This isn't exactly one to remember. Patrik Berger crosses hard and low, beating goalkeeper John Filan, and the ball strikes Gabby before just about rolling over the line. But who cares? As they say, it doesn't matter how you score as long as the ball goes in.

10. SHEFFIELD UNITED (h) 3-0

Shrugging off a challenge from Matthew Kilgallon, Gabby unleashes a magnificent angled drive which flies past goalkeeper Paddy Kenny and into the far corner. It's a magnificent strike which would have beaten any keeper.

GABBY CELEBRATES WITH THE HOLTE END AFTER SCORING THE VITAL EQUALISER AGAINST EVERTON

GABBY AND LIAM RIDGEWELL FIND A QUIET CORNER TO CELEBRATE AT STAMFORD BRIDGE

21

THE NAME GAME

SEE IF YOU CAN YOU UNRAVEL THESE ANAGRAMS TO UNRAVEL THE NAMES OF VILLA PLAYERS...

1. CHEW ON JAR **** *****

2. YOU SHY ANGEL ****** *****

3. SLAY ONE HUMAN ***** *******

4. ANY OVER... SPLIT IT ******** *******

5. KITER GRAB REP ****** ******

6. SUMATRAN LINER ****** *******

7. BELL FROM LEGO **** ********

8. GRAB HER TRAY ****** *****

9. I.O.U. A HORSE BASIN ****** ********

10. GRADING CARER ***** ******

If you get stuck the answers are on page 61

If you get stuck the answers are on page 61

Martin O'Neill

Getting to know the boss!

Born: Kilrea, Northern Ireland, 1st March 1952.

Playing career: Norwich City, Nottingham Forest, Manchester City.

Honours: FOREST – League champions 1978; League Cup winners 1978, 1979; European Cup winners 1980.

Managerial career: Stamford, Shepshed, Wycombe Wanderers, Norwich City, Leicester City, Celtic, Villa.

Honours:
WYCOMBE – FA Trophy 1991; Conference champions 1993; Promoted from Third Division, 1994.

LEICESTER – League Cup winners 1997, 2000; Promoted from First Division 2001

CELTIC – SPL champions 2001, 2002, 2004; Scottish Cup – 2001, 2004, 2005; Scottish League Cup 2001; UEFA Cup finalists 2003.

SQUAD
SNAPSHOTS

Thomas Sorensen

Born: ROMFORD, 28/11/80
Position: GOALKEEPER
Signed: JUNE 2005
Debut: MANCHESTER CITY (a)
31/10/05, Premiership
Previous club: ARSENAL

2006-07 record:
Appearances – 4(2 sub) league,
1 cup

Born: FREDERECIA, DENMARK,
12/06/76
Position: GOALKEEPER
Signed: AUGUST2003
Debut: PORTSMOUTH (a)
16/08/03, Premiership
Previous clubs: ODENSE BK,
SUNDERLAND

2006-07 record:
Appearances – 29 league, 2 cup

Stuart Taylor

Born: HAVERFORDWEST, 13/05/76
Position: RIGHT-BACK
Signed: MARCH 1999
Debut: NOTTINGHAM FOREST (h) 24/09/99, Premiership
Previous club: CARDIFF CITY

2006-07 record:
Appearances - 0

Mark Delaney

Born: AMNCHARAD, SWEDEN, 03/09/77
Position: CENTRAL DEFENDER
Signed: JULY 2001
Debut: TOTTENHAM (a) 18/08/00, Premiership
Previous clubs: DAGEFORS, AIK STOCKHOLM, RACING SANTANDER

2006-07 record:
Appearances – 38 league, 3 cup
Goals – 1 league

Olof Mellberg

Martin Laursen

Born: SILKEBORG, DENMARK, 26/07/76
Position: CENTRAL DEFENDER
Signed: MAY 2004
Debut: SOUTHAMPTON (h) 14/08/04, Premiership
Previous clubs: SILKEBORG, VERONA, PARMA, AC MILAN

2006-07 record:
Appearances – 12 (2 sub) league, 1 cup

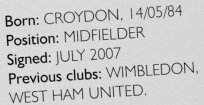

Born: CROYDON, 14/05/84
Position: MIDFIELDER
Signed: JULY 2007
Previous clubs: WIMBLEDON, WEST HAM UNITED.

Nigel Reo-Coker

Born: LONDON, 21/07/85
Position: CENTRAL DEFENDER
Signed pro: DECEMBER 2002
Debut: BLACKBURN (h) 04/01/03, FA Cup
Previous clubs: None

2006-07 record:
Appearances – 19 (2 sub) league, 3 cup Goals – 1 league

Liam Ridgewell

Gary Cahill

Born: SHEFFIELD, 19/12/85
Position: CENTRAL DEFENDER
Signed pro: DECEMBER 2003
Debut: WYCOMBE WANDERERS
(a) 20/09/05, League Cup
Previous clubs: None

2006-07 record:
Appearances – 19 (1 sub) league,
1 cup

Born: PRAGUE, CZECH
REPUBLIC, 10/11/73
Position: MIDFIELDER
Signed: JULY 2005

Debut: BLACKBURN ROVERS (h)
17/09/05, Premiership
Previous clubs: SLAVIA PRAGUE,
BORUSSIA DORTMUND,
LIVERPOOL, PORTSMOUTH

2006-07 record:
Appearances – 5 (8 sub) league,
0 (1sub) cup
Goals – 2 league

Patrik Berger

Gareth Barry

Stiliyan Petrov

Born: LONDON, 25/08/79
Position: STRIKER
Signed: JULY 2007
Previous clubs:
NOTTINGHAM FOREST,
WEST HAM UNITED.

Marlon Harewood

Born: BIRMINGHAM, 25/11/86
Position: MIDFIELDER
Signed pro: JANUARY 2005
Debut: EVERTON (h) 26/12/05,
Premiership
Previous clubs: None

2006-07 record:
Appearances – 11 (2 sub) league
Goals – 2 league

Craig Gardner

Shaun Maloney

Born: MALAYSIA, 24/01/83
Position: MIDFIELDER
Signed: JANUARY 2007
Debut: READING (a) 10/02/07
Previous club: CELTIC

2006-07 record:
Appearances – 5 (3 sub) league
Goals – 1 league

Born: STEVENAGE, 09/07/85
Position: WINGER
Signed: JANUARY 2007
Debut: NEWCASTLE (a) 31/01/07
Previous club: WATFORD

2006-07 record:
Appearances – 11 (2 sub) league
Goals – 2 league

Ashley Young

John Carew

Born: NORWAY, 05/09/79
Position: STRIKER
Signed: JANUARY 2007
Debut: NEWCASTLE (a) 31/01/07
Previous clubs: VALERNGEN, ROSENBORG, TRONDHEIM, VALENCIA, AS ROMA (loan), BESIKTAS, LYON.

2006-07 record:
Appearances – 11 league
Goals – 3 league

Born: BIRMINGHAM, 13/02/86
Position: STRIKER
Signed pro: FEBRUARY 2003
Debut: BIRMINGHAM CITY (h)
22/02/04, Premiership
Previous clubs: None

2006-07 record:
Appearances – 7 (6 sub) league,
1 cup
Goals – 4 league

Luke Moore

Born: BIRMINGHAM, 13/10/86
Position: STRIKER
Signed pro: FEBRUARY 2005
Debut: EVERTON (a) 18/03/05
Previous clubs: None

2006-07 record:
Appearances – 37 (1 sub)
league, 4 cup
Goals – 9 league, 1 cup

Gabriel Agbonlahor

A spot-on dozen!

Gareth Barry has a simple piece of advice for any youngster stepping up to take a penalty for his school team: "Don't worry if you have an attack of nerves."

Villa's captain knows all about feeling butterflies in his stomach when he steps up to try and beat an opposition goalkeeper from 12 yards — because it happens every time!

" IT'S ALWAYS A NERVOUS SITUATION, WHETHER IT'S YOUR FIRST PENALTY OR YOUR 50TH"
GARETH BARRY

"It's a one-on-one with the goalkeeper and all eyes are on you," he says.

"But it's not a bad thing to be nervous in a situation like that. It can help you focus."

Gareth certainly had plenty of opportunity to focus last season. Villa were awarded 10 penalties — more than in any other Premiership campaign — and he took eight of them.

He had a pretty good success rate, too, scoring six and missing two, both of which were saved by the goalkeeper.

And those six conversions meant he joined an elite Villa club.

Already one of only 34 players to have made more than 300 competitive appearances for Villa, he is now one of only 13 in the club's history to have scored 10 or more spot kicks.

Eric Houghton, who played for Villa in the 1930s and was manager when we won the FA Cup in 1957, is top of the chart with an incredible 58, although Gareth has a long way to go to match that. His total at the end of 2006-07 was a more modest 12 – but it's still an achievement to be one of such a small group of players to have reached double figures with their penalty conversions.

HERE ARE GARETH'S SUCCESSES TO THE END OF LAST SEASON:

Opponents	Result	Date	Goalkeeper
CELTA VIGO (IT)	1-2	02/08/00	JOSE PINTO
Portsmouth	1-2	16/08/03	SHAKA HISLOP
Newcastle	3-0	02/04/05	SHAY GIVEN
Newcastle	3-0	02/04/05	SHAY GIVEN
Tottenham	1-5	01/05/05	PAUL ROBINSON
Wycombe (LC)	8-3	20/09/05	FRANK TALIA
FULHAM	1-1	21/10/06	ANTTI NIEMI
Leicester City (LC)	3-2	24/10/06	PAUL HENDERSON
BLACKBURN	2-0	05/11/06	BRAD FRIEDEL
MIDDLESBROUGH	1-1	25/11/06	MARK SCHWARZER
Portsmouth	2-2	02/12/06	DAVID JAMES
Charlton Athletic	1-2	30/12/06	SCOTT CARSON

IT – InterToto Cup; LC – League Cup

LOCAL HERO!

Every player takes enormous pride in pulling on the famous claret and blue Villa shirt – and it's extra special for someone who grew up supporting the club. Just ask midfielder CRAIG GARDNER, who was brought up in Yardley.

1. WHEN DID YOU FIRST COME TO VILLA PARK, AND WHO BROUGHT YOU?

I can't remember exactly when it was, but it was with my older brothers Carl, Terry and Mark, who were already hooked on Villa. I was maybe seven or eight.

2. WHAT CAN YOU REMEMBER OF YOUR EARLY VISITS TO GAMES?

The biggest thing that struck me was that we had to stand up – we stood on the Holte End when it was still a massive terrace. It became all-seater at the end of that season.

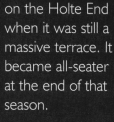

3. WHAT WAS YOUR FIRST VILLA REPLICA KIT?

It was a home shirt when the club were sponsored by Muller. I didn't really like the green black and white striped away shirt.

4. WHO WAS YOUR BOYHOOD HERO – AND WHY?

I heard all about what a great player Gordon Cowans was from my brothers but he'd left by the time I started watching Villa. My favourite at the time was Garry Parker because he had great composure and was such a good passer.

5. WHEN DID YOU JOIN THE VILLA ACADEMY?

When I was 14. I was spotted by a scout called Arthur Corbett, playing for the District schools' team and I started in Villa's under-15s.

6. WHAT HONOURS HAVE YOU WON SO FAR?

We were Academy League under-17 champions in 2004. We finished top of our group and then knocked out Sheffield United and Blackburn in the play-offs before beating Everton 6-2 on aggregate in the final. I scored one of the goals when we beat them 5-1 at Villa Park in the first leg. We also reached the FA Youth Cup final that year, losing to Middlesbrough.

7. TELL US ABOUT YOUR FIRST TEAM DEBUT.

It was Boxing Day, 2005, at home to Everton. It was an incredible feeling, running on to the pitch in front of so many people – a dream come true, really. Thankfully, there wasn't too much pressure because Villa were 3-0 up when I went on, and Milan Baros made it 4-0 a minute later!

8. WHAT'S YOUR BEST MOMENT SO FAR IN CLARET AND BLUE?

That has to be scoring my first goal for the first team in last season's 3-1 win at Middlesbrough. It was nearly half-time and we were one-down but when Gabby Agbonlahor knocked the ball in from the right, I was able to control it quickly and hit it past Mark Schwarzer. What a feeling!

9. WHAT'S YOUR BIGGEST AMBITION?

To be a regular in the Villa team – and I wouldn't mind playing for England, either!

10. WHAT DOES IT MEAN TO YOU TO BE A VILLA PLAYER?

Everything. I supported them as a boy and came up through the youth teams. Now my mates come and cheer me on!

MARTIN
LAURSEN

QUIZ TIME

How much can you remember about last season? Hercules has compiled a few questions to test your knowledge. Most of the answers can be found in the Review of the Season but see how many you can answer without looking!

1. Who scored Villa's first goal of 2006-07?

2. Manager Martin O'Neill wasn't the only new arrival to have won the European Cup with Nottingham Forest. Name the other one.

3. Which three Villa players played for England under-21s in the first game at the new Wembley Stadium?

4. Which striker left the club to play for New York Red Bulls?

5. Three players scored their first Villa goals during the month of April. Who were they?

6. Which player took over from Olof Mellberg as captain?

7. Ashley Young scored on his debut and John Carew was on target on his home debut four days later. Who were Villa's opponents in those two games?

8.Which team ended Villa's 11-match unbeaten start to the season?

9. What is the nationality of the club's new owners?

10. Who scored Villa's fastest goal of the season?

How did you get on? See page 60 for the answers.

WILFRED
BOUMA

Can you find your way to Villa Park? It has been raining so watch out for the slippery mud, and footballs blocking your path. Answer is on page 61.

START

VILLA PARK

Little & Large!

They have quickly become known as Little & Large – and you don't have to be a rocket scientist to realise why.

At 6ft 4in, John Carew is one of the tallest players ever to pull on a Villa shirt. At 5ft 10in, Ashley Young isn't exactly one of the shortest, although he admits it feels that way when he looks up at Big John.

But if they are at different ends of the height scale, they also have a lot in common.

They signed for Villa at the same time and made their debuts on the same night, immediately forging a good understanding.

And while Young was on target in that game against Newcastle United at St.James' Park, Carew scored on his home debut against West Ham a few days later – with Young providing the pass.

The duo combined well again against Manchester City at Eastlands later in the season, Carew heading Villa's first goal from a centre by his little mate!

"John and I struck up a good relationship straight away," says Ashley. "We signed on the same day and clicked straight away on the pitch. You can learn a lot off someone like John, who has played in the Champions League and has done well throughout his career."

Apart from their size, the only major difference between the duo is how they arrived at Villa Park.

This is only Ashley's second club after he effectively grew up as a player at Watford, while John could hardly be more widely travelled.

Having started his career in his homeland Norway with Valerngen, Rosenborg and Trondheim, he has since played in Spain (for Valencia), Italy (on loan to AS Roma), Turkey (Besiktas) and France (Lyon).

Ashley, by the way, has some good advice for youngsters with dreams of playing top level football – don't give up, even if you are told you're not good enough.

Having been on Watford's books since the age of 10, he was told he wasn't going to make the grade, but never lost faith in his own ability.

"They said I could either leave, or stay on and do some part-time work and some training," he explains.

"I decided to do that because I felt I could make it. I wanted to show them what they would be missing if I left.

"It worked out very well for me because I ended up getting my first professional contract. Now I want to show Watford what they are missing by doing well for Villa."

John Carew
scores against
West Ham and
team-mate
Ashley Young
joins in the
celebrations.

GARETH BARRY

SPOT THE BALL

Using your football skills, can you spot where the ball is in this picture?

SPOT THE DIFFERENCE

There are five differences in the fans picture below, can you spot what they are?

See page 60 for the answers.

SIDEWAYS

It's nothing out of the ordinary for small groups of young supporters and their parents to gather at Villa's training ground to watch their favourite players preparing for the next match.

But when the club staged an Open Training Session at Villa Park, around 3,000 people turned up to witness the event.

The fans saw Martin O'Neill's men going through their warm-up routines of stretching, jogging and sprinting before being treated to a game lasting 15 minutes each way.

But rather than the goal posts being in their usual positions in front of the Holte End and the North Stand, they were located in front of the Trinity Road and Doug Ellis stands.

It was certainly strange to watch the action taking place across the pitch rather than up and down it, but no-one seemed to mind as supporters enjoyed a rare opportunity to watch Villa training inside the stadium.

"It was a good idea to bring the fans in and let them see the work we do," said the manager. "It was a bit of fun and a change of venue for the players."

A few lucky competition winners also had the chance to meet their heroes in the tunnel, while others had the opportunity to take penalties against goalkeepers Thomas Sorensen and Robert Olejnik.

And just in case any of our very young fans got bored, the club's mascots Hercules and Bella were on hand to keep them entertained!

WHO SAID IT?

Here's a test of what you remember about last season from the things Villa's players said. To give you a start, the first comment was made by Ashley Young, so the answer is 1A. Now it's your turn to match the other players with their quotes!

1. When I was a kid, Ian Wright was my favourite player and I modelled myself on him. These days I'm a big fan of Thierry Henry, so it would be nice to think I could combine the best qualities of those two.

2. I think Gareth can do a good job. It gave me a lift when I was given the captaincy and I'm sure it will be the same for him. It's something to be proud of.

3. I talked to Martin O'Neill for 10 minutes and then went to Bulgaria, where I signed my contract and sent it back by fax.

4. I was delighted to score on my debut at Everton last season, even though we lost. But to score at Villa Park was a dream come true.

5. I had a bit of stick from Tottenham supporters behind the goal. They were shouting 'Arsenal reject' but that's something you expect. It's just part of the game.

6. It's worth nothing to say I was bought from AC Milan for a lot of money if I don't perform well.

7. I jumped at the chance. It's not every day you're asked to be captain of a club with so much tradition.

8. I had a few awards when I was at PSV but it was really pleasing to get one here.

9. It was an amazing experience. Wembley was absolutely magnificent and it was superb to represent my country there for my debut.

10. The Celtic support is unique but since I've been here I've been really impressed with the Villa fans.

THE PLAYERS
A. ASHLEY YOUNG
B. GARY CAHILL
C. WILFRED BOUMA
D. GARETH BARRY
E. OLOF MELLBERG
F. MARTIN LAURSEN
G. STUART TAYLOR
H. GABBY AGBONLAHOR
I. SHAUN MALONEY
J. STILIYAN PETROV

If you get stuck the answers are on page 60

49

JUNIOR VILLANS

WELL DONE HARRY!

The Villa rap

Ten-year-old Nicola Bywater has combined her love of Villa and her talent as a poet to produce The Aston Villa Rap. See what you think!

Aston Villa are the best,
All their supporters are full of zest.
The manager is Martin O'Neill,
And for us he's a very big deal.
Everyone loves Agbonlahor,
He's the best player that's come through the door.

Ashley Young, he came to us,
And all the fans made such a fuss.
Then along came John Carew,
Now you'll see what Villa can do.
Just to make it very clear –
We're heading up the table this year!

Harry's game

What do you do if you can't find the latest issue of the **Villa News & Record?** You make your own copy!

At least, that's what Harry Rai did. Six-year-old Harry compiled a 26-page programme – all hand-written and drawn – during his school lunch breaks.

He was unable to play outside because he had broken his foot, so he turned his attention to the two things he likes best – Aston Villa and football programmes!

Kate's a winner

Everyone had a good time at the club's Open Training Session – but Kate Hughes enjoyed the day more than most.

She had the chance to meet manager Martin O'Neill after winning a competition on the club's official website www.avfc.co.uk.

John's top draw

At the age of 11, Matt Bouttell is showing plenty of artistic temperament.

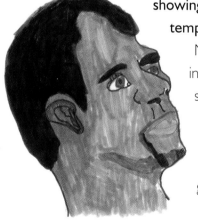

Matt drew and coloured in this excellent portrait of striker John Carew – and the Norwegian striker reckoned the youngster had managed a pretty good likeness!

Bethany's viewpoint

Villa's lioness mascot Bella caught up with nine-year-old Bethany Wardle in the Trinity Road stand family section.

But although that is where Bethany now has her season ticket, she visited all four sides of Villa Park before deciding on her favourite viewing position.

She came to Villa Park for the first time in 2002 for the match against Derby, when she was five. Since then, she and her dad Nathan have sat in both the North Stand and Doug Ellis stand.

Well, they do say women (and young ladies) have the right to change their minds!

Hercules' view

No doubt you've heard of a bird's eye view or a worm's eye view. Well, here's a lion's eye view!

If you have ever wondered where club mascot Hercules goes once he has provided his pre-match entertainment, we can reveal the answer.

Like any other Villa fan, our loveable lion likes to watch the match – usually with members of the ground staff in the corner between the Holte End and the Doug Ellis stand.

Join the club!

Junior Villans is the club for all claret and blue nuts up to the age of 16.

Check out the section for your age group (or get mum or dad to do it for you) and you will be joining a special Villa club designed just for you.

And all new members receive a voucher which can be spent in the Villa Village Megastore!

VILLA CUBS (0-5 years)
Become a Junior Villan from birth by joining the Villa Cubs – a perfect start to becoming a claret and blue devotee.

VILLA LIONS (6-12 years)
Join the Villa Lions and you won't just roar on the boys with the rest of the crowd, you will have the chance to lead your heroes on to the pitch as a mascot!

VILLA TEENS (13-16 years)
Join Villa Teens at 13 and continue to enjoy the benefits of the Junior Villans. You will have the chance to take part in question-and-answer sessions with the players – so start thinking what you would like to ask!

Membership for any of the three clubs runs for 12 months from your date of enrolment.

You will receive newsletters, a Christmas card and a surprise gift, a birthday card and a 10 per cent discount at the club's stores in the Villa Village and Pavilion Central.

There's free admission to reserve home games for all members – and all Junior Villans can go free to our popular Kickin' Kids parties.

To enroll, call 0800 6120970, or e-mail: hercules@avfc.co.uk.

What do you know about
Villa?

1 From which club did Ashley Young join Villa?

A) Watford ☐   B) Wolves ☐   C) Reading ☐

2 In which year was Villa formed?
A) 1872 ☐   B) 1874 ☐   C) 1888 ☐

3 Against which club did John Carew score on his home debut?
A) Newcastle ☐   B) West Ham ☐   C) Bolton ☐

4 How many penalties did Gareth Barry score last season?

A) Four ☐
B) Five ☐
C) Six ☐

5 Which player has made most Premiership appearances for the club?
A) Alan Wright ☐   B) Gareth Barry ☐
C) Olof Mellberg ☐

6 Who is the club's record goalscorer?
A) Billy Walker ☐   B) Harry Hampton ☐
C) Dwight Yorke ☐

7 How many times have Villa won the FA Cup?
A) Six ☐   B) Seven ☐   C) Eight ☐

8 Which team did we beat in the 1996 League Cup final?
A) Man United ☐   B) Chelsea ☐   C) Leeds Utd ☐

9 Who was the club's manager immediately before Martin O'Neill?
A) Graham Taylor ☐   B) David O'Leary ☐   C) John Gregory ☐

10 How many times have we won the League Cup?
A) Three ☐   B) Four ☐   C) Five ☐

Dot-to-dot

Join the dots, in number order to reveal one of your favourite Villa mascots.

Guess who?

Can you guess which three players are, behind these clever disguises?

1.

2.

3.

V	I	L	L	A	Q	T	S	P	M
O	C	B	Z	L	K	C	B	T	O
R	H	G	A	R	D	N	E	R	O
T	A	Y	L	O	R	A	R	F	R
E	S	V	Y	O	U	N	G	D	E
P	D	A	V	I	S	U	E	B	Z
D	H	L	P	N	W	E	R	A	C
E	L	A	U	R	S	E	N	R	O
G	R	E	B	L	L	E	M	R	B
B	X	M	A	L	O	N	E	Y	T

Aston Villa wordsearch

Here's a chance to test your knowledge of Aston Villa. A total of 13 names are hidden in our word search. Some are horizontal, some are vertical and some go backwards. The names you should find are:

VILLA	**PETROV**
CAREW	**BARRY**
YOUNG	**BERGER**
MALONEY	**GARDNER**
LAURSEN	**MOORE**
MELLBERG	**DAVIS**
TAYLOR	

THOMAS SORENSEN

It's a real Aston mess

Here's a recipe for young Villa supporters with a sweet tooth. There's no cooking involved, and it tastes as good as it looks. What's more, it can be enjoyed the following day!

If you use the quantities suggested, you will be able to treat yourself and five friends to a big helping of Aston Mess!

What you will need

1 lb (450g) raspberries (washed and dried). (Save about 5 to decorate)

12 fl oz (375 ml) whipping cream

4 tablespoons sugar

8 tablespoons rolled or porridge oats

A few sprigs of mint, blueberries or blackberries to decorate (optional).

What to do

1. Mash the raspberries in a large bowl with a fork, so that they are still a bit lumpy.

2. Put the cream into another bowl, and whip until thick.

3. Now add the cream to the raspberries, add the sugar, and mix gently.

4. Add the oats, and mix lightly until the raspberries start to turn the mixture pink.

5. Cover and place in the fridge to chill for one hour (if you can leave it alone for that long!).

6. Serve in bowls, and decorate.

MARTIN OPENS THE
NEW TRAINING
GROUND

Inside Bodymoor Heath

A top class training camp is no guarantee of success – but it can be a big help. And there's no doubt that Villa now have one of the best training grounds in the world.

The new £13m complex, officially opened by manager Martin O'Neill, was brought into use at the start of the season after the club realised the original building, built back in 1971, had become outdated. It's only a few hundred yards from the old building to the new, but they are light years apart in terms of facilities.

Let us take you on a whistle-stop tour of the amenities which are available to Villa's players and backroom staff at the new two-storey building:

The first team dressing room is the height of luxury, with its huge lockers and underfloor heating, and there are separate changing areas for the reserves and youth teams – plus a further eight dressing rooms for under-nines through to under-16s.

There's a sauna and steam rooms, a swimming pool, hot and cold plunge pools – plus a hydrotherapy pool to help players recovering from injury.

Inside the massive gym, you will find all the latest fitness equipment and there is also a rehabilitation area.

The ground floor has offices for the chairman, secretary and manager, plus the players' welfare officer, the coaching staff and Academy staff.

Upstairs, we have the players' lounge, restaurant, snooker hall and computer room, which doubles as a press room.

Behind the main building is a massive "barn" which includes a 70m running track.

One of the three new pitches, which should be ready for the start of the 2008-09 season, will be an exact replica of the Villa Park surface, right down to the size, the type of grass and even the camber.

The complex is completed by an all-weather pitch, warm-up and goalkeeping areas, a laundry area and a one-mile outdoor track.

2007 - onwards

Villa's badge has, for many years, been an integral part of kit worn by the club's players, and we kicked off the 2007-08 season with a completely new design.

In many ways, we have gone back to the future, because the new badge has a much more traditional look than the one it has replaced.

Here are a few key factors which resulted in the latest design, so be sure to impress your friends with the inside story of how the new badge came into being!

• The heraldic shape is a throwback to a bygone age and mirrors a family coat of arms. Quite simply, we want everyone connected with Villa to feel part of the family.

• After being omitted from the previous badge, the letters AVFC have been re-introduced. We should never let anyone forget we are a football club.

• The fragmented lion has been replaced by an animal with a fuller figure – signalling a desire for togetherness within the club and among supporters.

• Gone is the striped background, replaced by a solid blue which represents honesty and loyalty.

• The word Prepared has been retained because it is the club's motto. Villa are prepared to meet every challenge, both on and off the pitch.

• It's only a small change, but that little white star glows brightly as a reminder of the greatest night in Villa's history. No matter how young you are, it's important that every Villa fan is aware that we won the European Cup in 1982.

More than anything, let's hope the new badge helps us back to our former glories!

1940s - 1950s

1950s - 1960s

1970s - 1990s

1990s - 2007

HOW DID YOU

Quick quiz answers to p37

1. Olof Mellberg
2. Assistant manager John Robertson
3. Ashley Young, Gary Cahill and Gabby Agbonlahor
4. Juan Pablo Angel
5. Patrik Berger, Craig Gardner and Shaun Maloney
6. Gareth Barry
7. Newcastle and West Ham
8. Liverpool
9. American
10. Stiliyan Petrov

Who said it?

1. A   2. E   3. J   4. H   5. G
6. F   7. D   8. C   9. B   10. I

Answers to p49

Spot the difference p43

1. Yellow face paint
2. Green hair
3. Star on glasses
4. Green face paint
5. Red glasses

Spot the ball p43   Answer E5

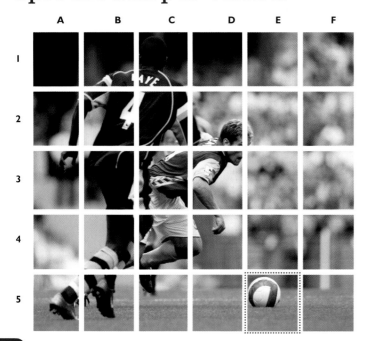

GET ON?

Can you find your way to Villa Park?

START

VILLA PARK

Answer to p39

The name game

1. John Carew
2. Ashley Young
3. Shaun Maloney
4. Stiliyan Petrov
5. Patrik Berger
6. Martin Laursen
7. Olof Mellberg
8. Gareth Barry
9. Isaiah Osbourne
10. Craig Gardner

Answers to p22

Word search p53

V	I	L	L	A	Q	T	S	P	M
O	C	B	Z	L	K	C	B	T	O
R	H	G	A	R	D	N	E	R	O
T	A	Y	L	O	R	A	R	F	R
E	S	V	Y	O	U	N	G	D	E
P	D	A	V	I	S	U	E	B	Z
D	H	L	P	N	W	E	R	A	G
E	L	A	U	R	S	E	N	R	O
G	R	E	B	L	L	E	M	R	B
B	X	M	A	L	O	N	E	Y	T

What do you know about Villa? p52

1. A) Watford
2. B) 1874
3. B) West Ham
4. C) Six
5. B) Gareth Barry
6. A) Billy Walker
7. B) Seven
8. C) Leeds Utd.
9. B) David O'Leary
10. C) Five

Guess who? p53

1. Gary Cahill
2. Shaun Maloney
3. John Carew

Every Villa supporter in a final day capacity crowd is given a free scarf, proclaiming the club's brand message: "Proud history – bright future."